Contents

What is a dog?

People in many countries like to keep pet dogs. Pet dogs are known as **domestic dogs**. They belong to a family of animals called the **canids**. Wolves, foxes and wild dogs are all members of this family.

▼ A pet dog can become an important part of the family.

Dogs have very good hearing. They also have a powerful sense of smell. Dogs can smell things that people cannot smell.

▲ Dogs sniff each other when they meet. This is how they get to know one another.

Dog Fact

Some types of dogs have a better sense of smell than others. These include bloodhounds and beagles.

Wild dogs

There are wild dogs in most parts of the world. Wolves and some wild dogs live and **hunt** in groups. These groups are called **packs**.

Dog Fact

About 15,000 years ago, some wolves began living with people. All pet dogs have come from these **tame** wolves.

▼ African wild dogs live in the grasslands of Africa.

▲ All pet dogs are related to the grey wolf, or timber wolf.

Domestic dogs

Dogs were the first animals to be kept by people. Dogs were very useful. They helped people to hunt. Dogs also made good guards and companions.

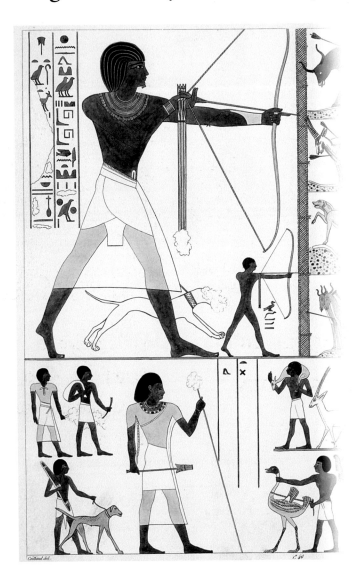

Dog Fact

There are about 600 million domestic dogs in the world.

◀ The ancient Egyptians kept dogs for hunting and as pets. This picture shows an Egyptian hunting scene.

Dogs that are well looked after can make wonderful pets. They will form strong bonds with their owners. Dogs can be very loving and playful.

▲ Dogs like to live in packs. To a pet dog, its owners are its pack.

A puppy is born

A young dog is called a **puppy**. A small mother dog can have up to six puppies in a **litter**. Bigger dogs can have as many as twelve. When they are born, the puppies are blind and deaf.

▼ For the first few weeks, puppies feed on their mother's milk.

A puppy's ears and eyes open when it is about two weeks old. By three weeks it can walk and **bark**. It can even wag its tail.

▲ Young puppies huddle together to keep warm.

Growing up

A puppy starts growing teeth when it is four weeks old. Now it can start to eat solid food. At eight weeks old, a puppy is ready to leave its mother.

▼ Young puppies need four or five small meals a day.

Dogs usually live for between twelve and fourteen years. Some types of dog have shorter lives. Others may live up to twenty years. Small dogs often live longer than large dogs.

▲ As they get old, dogs sleep more and eat less.

Dog Fact

A female dog is able to have puppies when she is six months old.

All sorts of dogs

There are many different types of dog.
Special types of dog are called **breeds**.
There are hundreds of different breeds.
Many dogs are a mix of breeds.

One of the tallest dogs is the Irish
Wolfhound. It can grow to be more
than 90 cm tall. The Chihuahua is one
of the smallest breeds.

▼ There are
many different
breeds of dog.
They come in all
shapes and sizes.

▼ This Great Dane towers over a Jack Russell terrier.

How dogs can help us

Some dogs are trained as guide dogs. They help blind people to get about. Police use specially trained dogs, too. They use sniffer dogs to sniff out drugs or **explosives**. They sometimes use tracker dogs to help them find people.

▼ Husky dogs are used to pull sleds through snow.

▼ This sheepdog is helping the farmer to herd and guard his sheep.

Choosing a pet dog

Only get a pet dog if you are sure you can give it lots of time and care. Then you can choose whether to have a puppy or an older dog. Rescue shelters have lots of dogs needing homes.

▼ These German Shepherd puppies will grow up to be large dogs. They will need lots of space and exercise.

Some people like **pedigree** dogs. These are dogs whose parents are of the same breed. Others prefer to have dogs that do not belong to any one breed.

▲ This dog is a mix of different breeds. Dogs like this are known as **mongrels**.

Caring for a dog

Your new pet will need to visit the vet for **vaccinations**. These are injections that will protect a dog against some serious diseases.

◀ All dogs should see a vet for a health check once a year.

Dogs need at least two meals a day and water to drink to stay healthy. Dried or tinned dog food gives them the goodness they need. Bones or chews will help keep their teeth strong.

▲ Dogs need to be brushed regularly. Sometimes they need to have baths.

Outdoor life

It is important to train your dog to behave well. You can do this by rewarding the dog when it does something right. Never hit or shout at your dog.

You will need to walk your dog at least twice a day. The exercise will help keep it fit, healthy and happy.

◀ Some people take their pets to dog training classes.

Your dog will love to play outdoor games with you.

Glossary

bark
A loud cry made by a dog.

breed
A special type of dog.

canids
Family of animals that includes dogs, wolves, foxes and jackals.

domestic dog
A dog that lives with people and is kept as a pet.

explosives
A substance or device that causes an explosion.

hunt
To chase and kill an animal for food.

litter
The offspring, or young, born to an animal at one time.

mongrel
A dog that does not belong to one breed.

pack
A group of animals, such as dogs, that live and hunt together.

pedigree
A type of dog whose parents were both of the same breed

puppy
A young dog.

tame
A wild animal that has become used to people.

vaccination
An injection that is given to protect people or animals against some serious diseases.

Index